HOW TO DRAW YOUR OWN GRAPHIC NOVEL

DRAWING THE HEROES IN YOUR GRAPHIC NOVEL

FRANK LEE

W
FRANKLIN WATTS
LONDON • SYDNEY

First published in 2012 by Franklin Watts

Franklin Watts
338 Euston Road
London NW1 3BH

Franklin Watts Australia
Level 17/207 Kent Street, Sydney, NSW 2000

Produced by Arcturus Publishing Limited,
26/27 Bickels Yard, 151–153 Bermondsey Street, London SE1 3HA

Text and illustrations: Frank Lee with Jim Hansen
Editors: Joe Harris and Kate Overy
Design: Andrew Easton
Cover design: Andrew Easton

A CIP catalogue record for this book is available from the British Library.

Dewey Decimal Classification Number 741.5'1

ISBN: 978 1 4451 1029 5

Printed in China

Franklin Watts is a division of Hachette Children's Books, an Hachette UK company.
www.hachette.co.uk

SL002069EN
Supplier 03, Date 0112, Print Run 1419

CONTENTS

Drawing Tools 4

What Makes a Hero? 6

Creating a Fantasy Hero 12

Creating a Superheroine 16

Creating a Sci-Fi Hero 20

Animated Heroes 24

Supporting Characters 28

Glossary 30

Further Reading 31

Websites 31

Index 32

DRAWING TOOLS

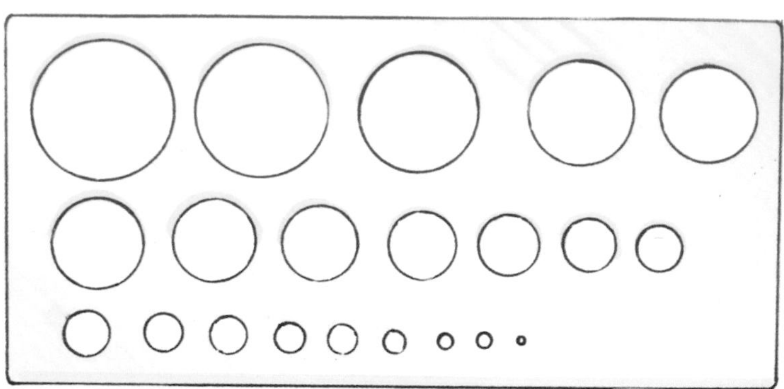

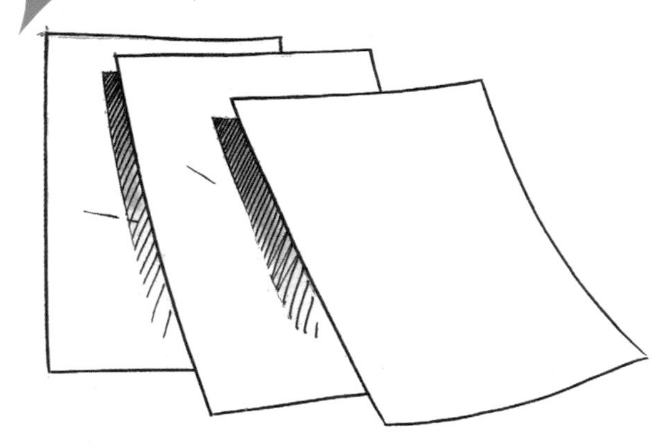

LAYOUT PAPER

Most professional illustrators use cheaper paper for basic layouts and practice sketches before they get around to the more serious task of producing a masterpiece on more costly paper. It's a good idea to buy some plain paper from a stationery shop for all your practice sketches. Go for the least expensive kind.

DRAWING PAPER

This is a heavy-duty, high-quality paper, ideal for your final version. You don't have to buy the most expensive brand. Most decent art or craft shops stock their own brand or a student brand and, unless you're thinking of turning professional, these will be fine.

WATERCOLOUR PAPER

This paper is made from 100 per cent cotton and is much higher quality than wood-based papers. Most art shops stock a large range of weights and sizes. Paper that is 300 gsm (140 lb) should be fine.

CIRCLE TEMPLATE

This is very useful for drawing small circles.

FRENCH CURVES

These are available in a few shapes and sizes and are useful for drawing curves.

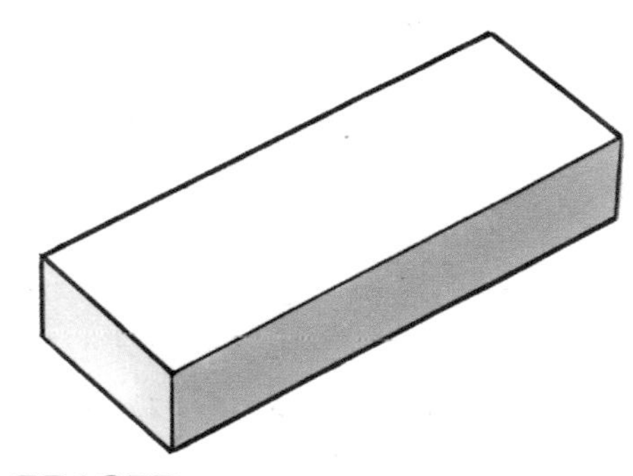

ERASER

There are three main types of eraser: rubber, plastic and putty. Try all three to see which kind you prefer.

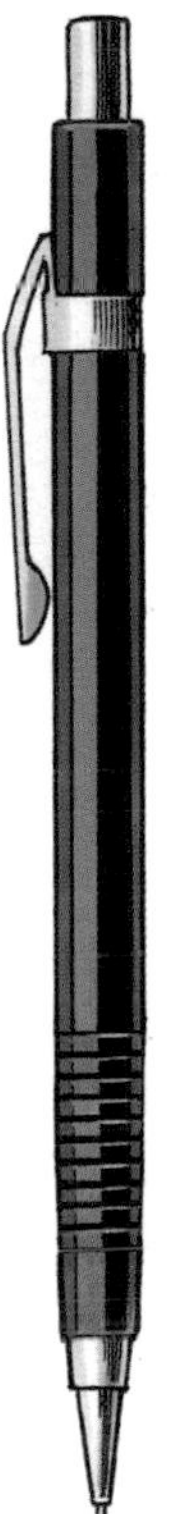

PENCILS

It's best not to cut corners on quality here. Get a good range of graphite (lead) pencils ranging from soft (B) to hard (2H).

Hard lead lasts longer and leaves less graphite on the paper. Soft lead leaves more lead on the paper and wears down more quickly. Every artist has their personal preference, but H pencils are a good medium range to start out with until you find your favourite.

Spend some time drawing with each weight of pencil and get used to their different qualities. Another good product to try is the mechanical pencil. These are available in a range of lead thicknesses, 0.5 mm being a good medium range. These pencils are very good for fine detail work.

PENS

There is a large range of good-quality pens on the market these days and all will do a decent job of inking. It's important to experiment with different pens to determine which you are most comfortable using.

You may find that you end up using a combination of pens to produce your finished artwork. Remember to use a pen that has waterproof ink if you want to colour your illustration with a watercolour or ink wash. It's a good idea to use one of these anyway. There's nothing worse than having your nicely inked drawing ruined by an accidental drop of water!

BRUSHES

Some artists like to use a fine brush for inking linework. This takes a bit more practice and patience to master, but the results can be very satisfying. If you want to try your hand at brushwork, you will definitely need to get some good-quality sable brushes.

MARKERS

These are very versatile pens and, with practice, can give pleasing results.

INKS

With the dawn of computers and digital illustration, materials such as inks have become a bit obscure, so you may have to look harder for these. Most good art and craft shops should stock them, though.

Heroes and heroines are at the centre of graphic-novel storytelling. They anchor the story and offer the reader inspiration, hope and escapism. Comic-book heroes offer a glimpse of a better world where justice prevails and good triumphs over evil.

When you create a character, you have to ask yourself: what sort of world do they live in? Is it a realm of sword and sorcery? A realistic, modern-day setting? A futuristic megacity? Or a completely new world of your own creation? There are no rules when it comes to creating your comic-book hero. The only limit is your own imagination!

BARBARIAN WARRIOR

You could choose to give your story a fantasy setting with a brave, powerful warrior as your hero. This guy would win the day by the might of his sword and his brutish strength. The fantasy art genre is filled with all sorts of interesting characters, from warriors and maidens to magical witches, wizards, orcs and elves. Take your pick!

Cyborg Commando

You could choose to set your story in the future, where advances in science and technology have reshaped the world. The cyborg is a futuristic hybrid between man and machine, a supersoldier with enhanced strength, speed and sight. Science fiction is very popular in comic books. Many superheroes owe their powers to freak accidents within the world of science fiction.

Caped Superhero

Will you choose a superhero to be at the centre of your story? Will he have the power of flight or be able to reach the tops of tall buildings in a single leap? Will he be faster than a speeding bullet or have mutant strength? Heroes with superpowers are made all the more interesting and complex if they have flaws or weaknesses that make them vulnerable and capable of being defeated or destroyed. What weakness might you give your superhero?

Masters of Magic

The mystical arts is another genre filled with fascinating characters. You could cast a warlock or wizard as your central character, like Doctor Darque (left). He is someone who has devoted his life to mastering the mystical arts and has the power to take on the forces of darkness. Alternatively your supernatural warrior could be a superhero with psychic powers such as telepathy and telekinesis, such as the Silver Sorceress (below).

Martial Artists

Why not give your story a martial-arts theme and fill it with characters who are experts in fighting techniques? Your hero could be a master in the many styles of kung fu or karate, having trained for many years in the art of combat. With arms of steel, this hero would pack a lightning-fast punch and kick harder than a horse. Such a skilful, stylish hero would be a tough opponent to defeat.

Real-Life Hero

Not all heroes are muscle-bound with superpowers. Some of the most captivating characters are just ordinary people who are thrown into extraordinary situations. Some heroes possess nothing more than fearless hearts to stand tall against the forces of evil and the intelligence to outwit their enemies.

Teen Hero

Perhaps your hero will be a teenager who must not only face great evil, but must also make their way through school. The cheerleader heroine in your story could secretly be a werewolf. Your hero could be a brilliant detective whom the police will never take seriously just because of his age. Teenagers make great heroes because they have yet to find their place in the world. Some of the most popular superheroes are teenagers who worry about bullies and dating as well as supervillains.

Western Hero

Yee-haw! You could choose to set your story in the pioneering days of America and include gunfights, horse chases and big, sweeping, untamed landscapes. There have been many heroes of the Wild West. It's not just the villains who may wish to conceal their identities. Perhaps your hero is someone who leads a dual life, a character who blends in with the crowd and tries not to draw attention to himself, but by night wages war on the corrupt and evil.

Good Cop

Crime comics offer a gritty realism where tough, cynical cops dish out justice to even tougher criminals. They live in cities that are overflowing with crime and corruption. Characters in this genre are often complex. Cops can be corrupt and criminals can have good hearts, making it hard to know whom to trust.

CREATING A FANTASY HERO

KRALL THE CONQUEROR

In this book you'll learn how to draw a variety of different heroes. You could choose to adapt and develop one of these figures to create your own central character. Even if you want your hero to look very different, the step-by-step technique you'll learn can be applied to any figure.

STEP 1

Establish the warrior's pose by drawing a stick figure, then add basic shapes to this frame. The warrior is strong and muscular, so we need to use bulky construction shapes.

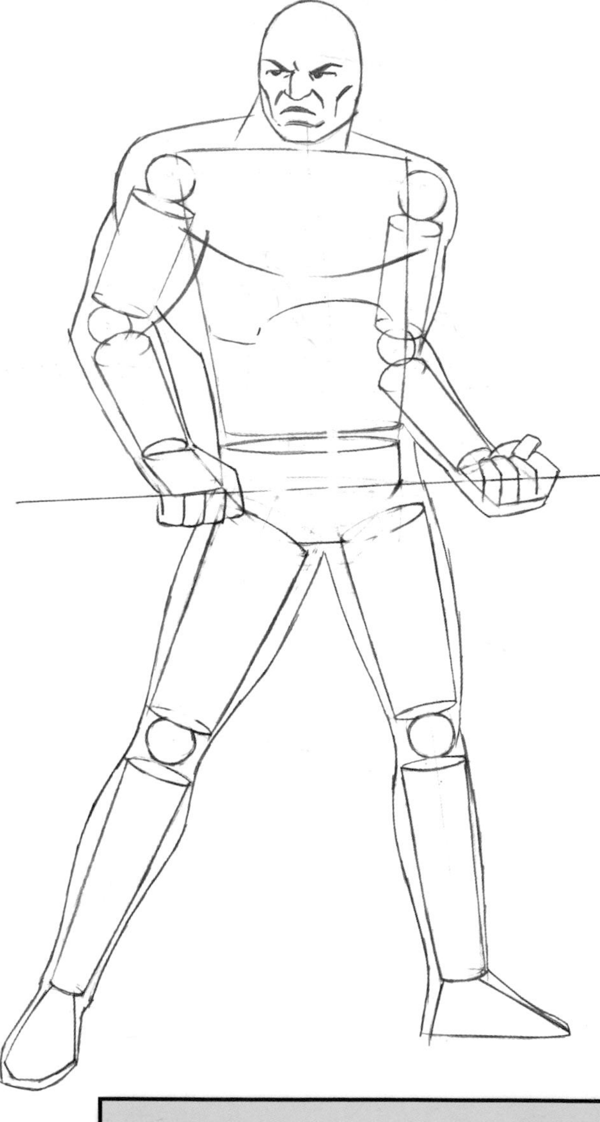

STEP 2

Draw his face and muscles. A strong, square jawline will suit this character. Draw around the construction shapes to create the outline of your figure.

STEP 3

Remove the basic shapes so you're left with a clean outline and begin to add detail. Draw the clothing, in this case an animal fur, a leather belt and a studded shoulder plate. Draw the warrior's mighty axe.

STEP 4

Clean up the pencil drawing and add any final details. Pencil in areas of light and shade to add depth to your drawing. This will look even more effective once it's inked.

STEP 5
Carefully apply ink over your pencil drawing.

STEP 6

The final step is to add colour. The key to successful colouring is to choose a limited colour palette that's not too complex. Here we have used earthy and neutral tones that all work together nicely.

CREATING A SUPERHEROINE

THE SILVER SORCERESS

This feisty superheroine is constructed using the same basic techniques as our male hero. She is shown with telekinetic energy glowing around her hands.

STEP 1

Start by drawing the basic stick figure. Female characters have smaller waists and narrower shoulders than males.

STEP 2

Draw an outline around the shapes to flesh out your figure. Draw the hands and map out the proportions of the face.

STEP 3
Add in the facial features, hair and clothing.

STEP 4
Erase your working lines and add final details. Draw the energy blasts she has conjured from the palms of her hands. She's ready for action!

STEP 5

Ink your character with clean, sharp lines.

STEP 6
Choose colours for your character's costume that will make your character stand out.

Creating a Sci-Fi Hero

Trooper X
You can really go wild with the design of science fiction characters. However, if you want your readers to relate to these heroes, they must still look recognizably human.

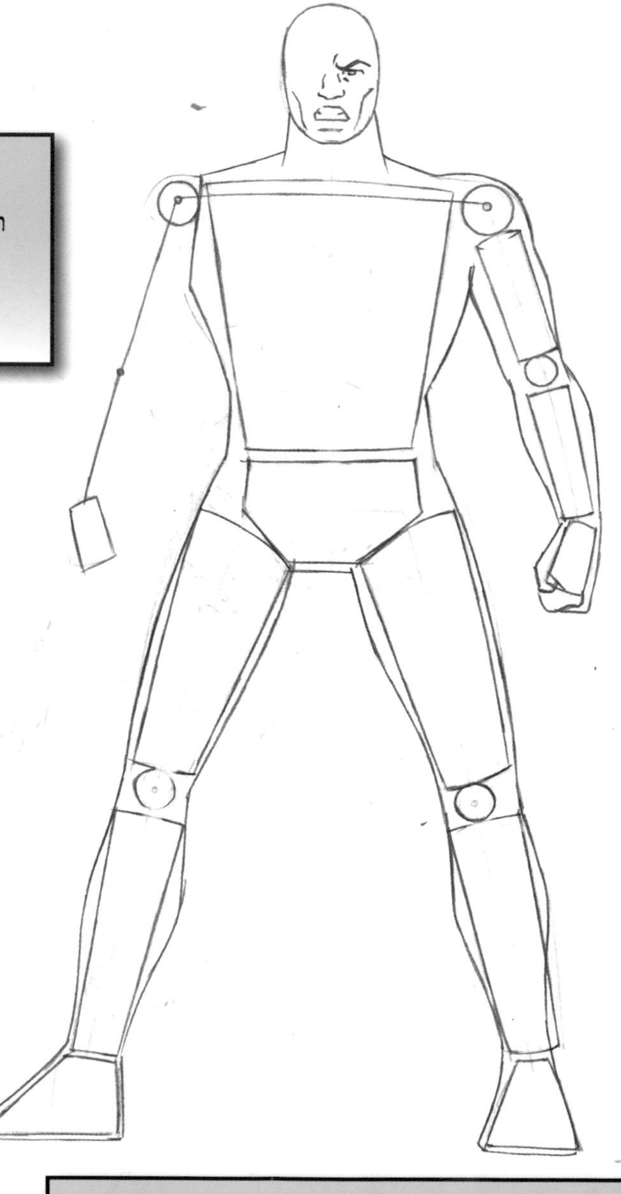

STEP 1
Construct the pose by drawing a stick figure and then add construction shapes. The cyborg has both feet firmly planted on the ground in this front-on pose.

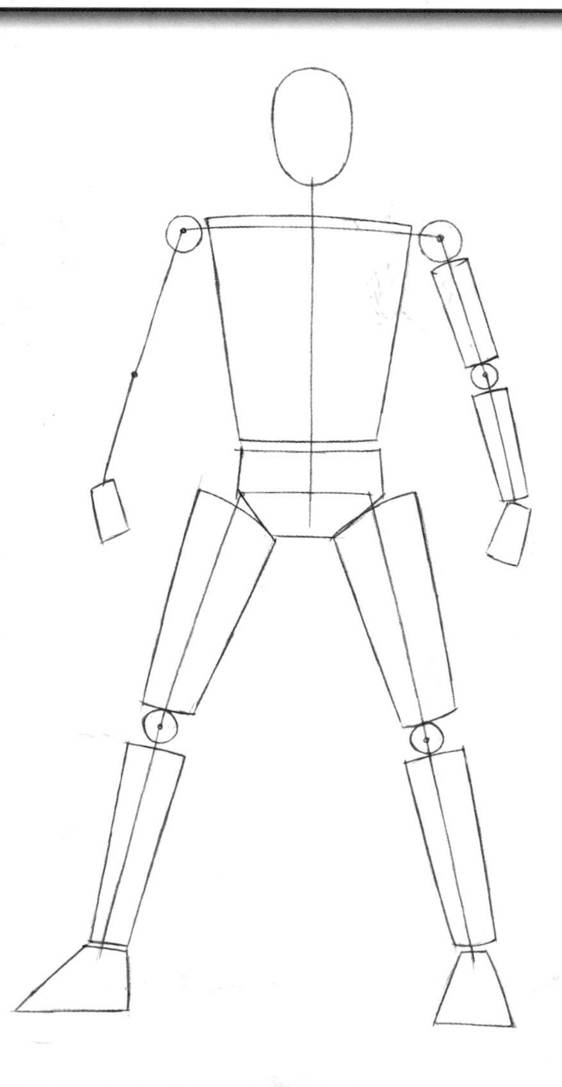

STEP 2
Using the construction shapes as a base, begin to define the muscle structure of this well-built hero. Start pencilling in the face.

STEP 3

Remove your working lines then pencil in the detail. Draw the cyborg's well-defined muscles and body armour. The two should merge together, as metal is as much a part of him as his flesh.

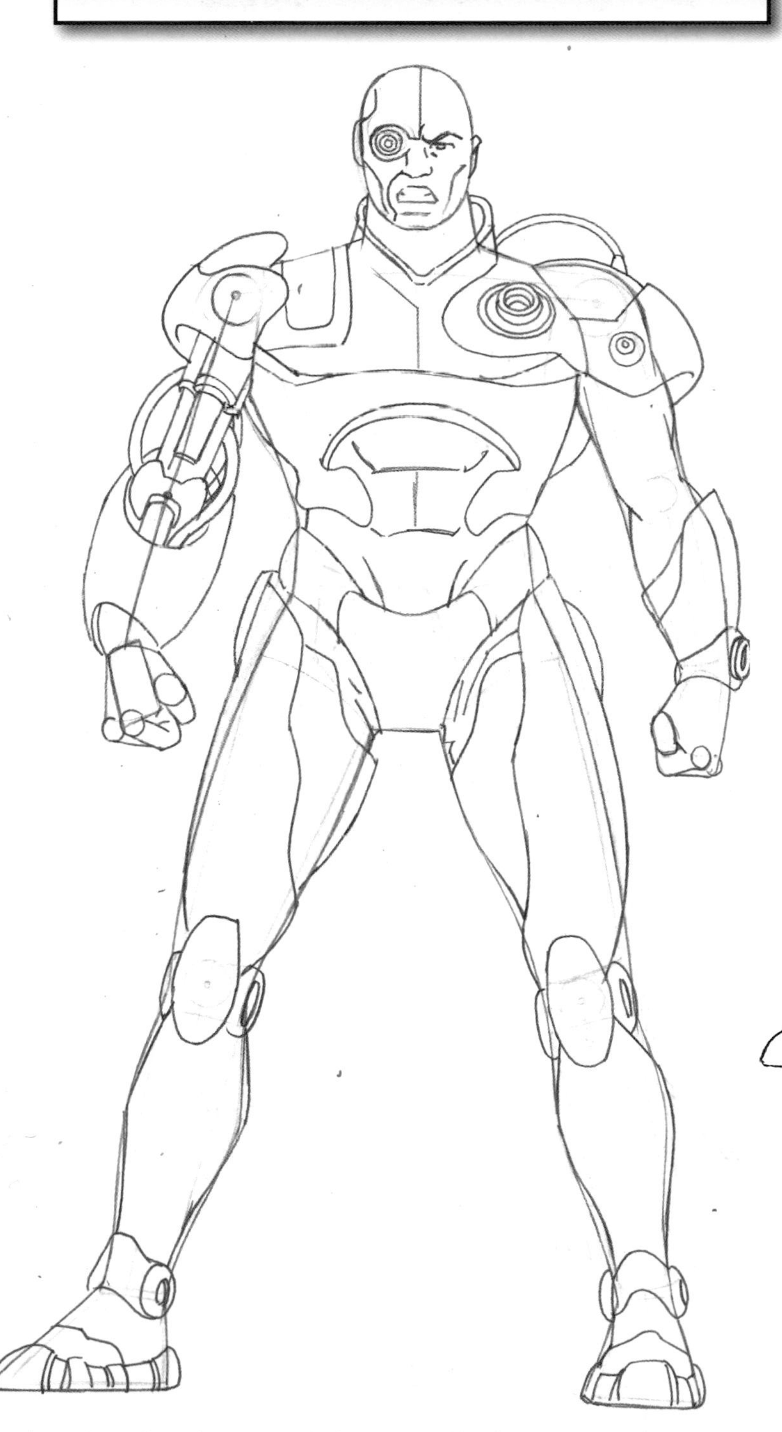

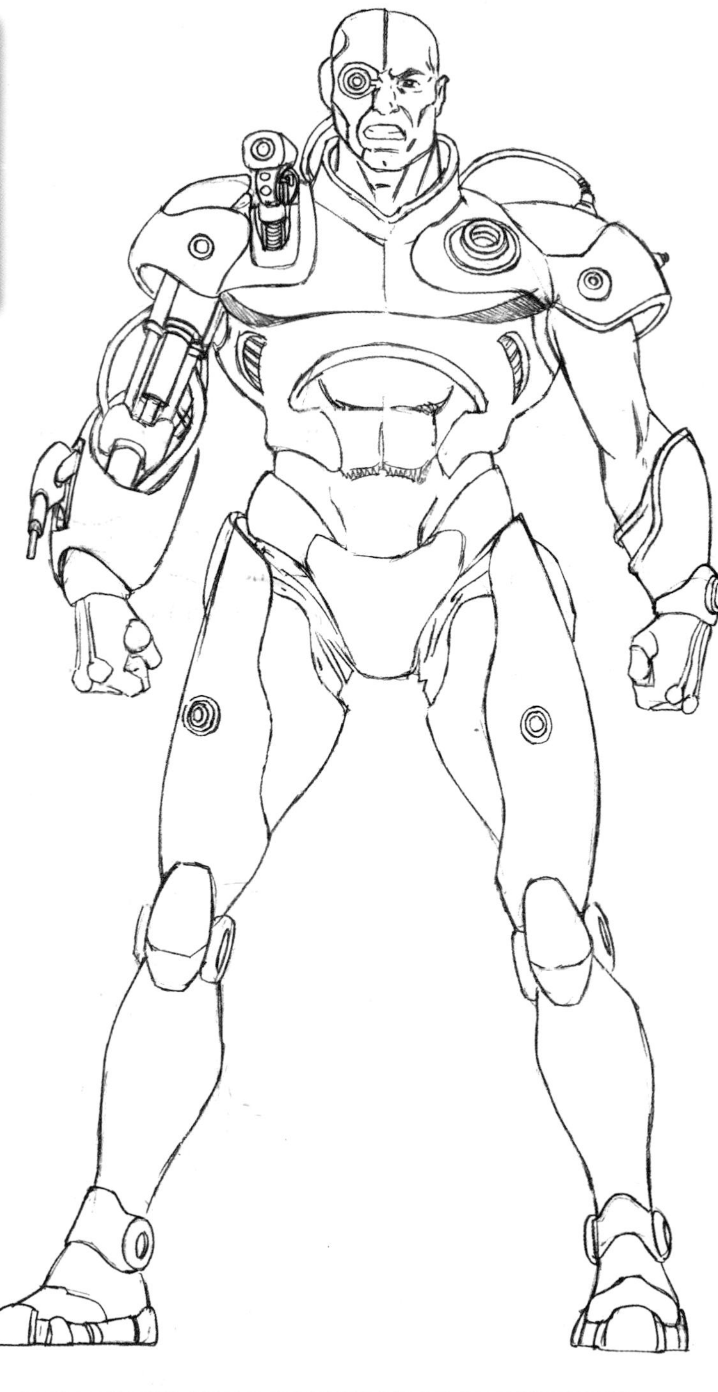

STEP 4

Add weaponry to the cyborg's armour to complete the pencil drawing and you're ready to start inking.

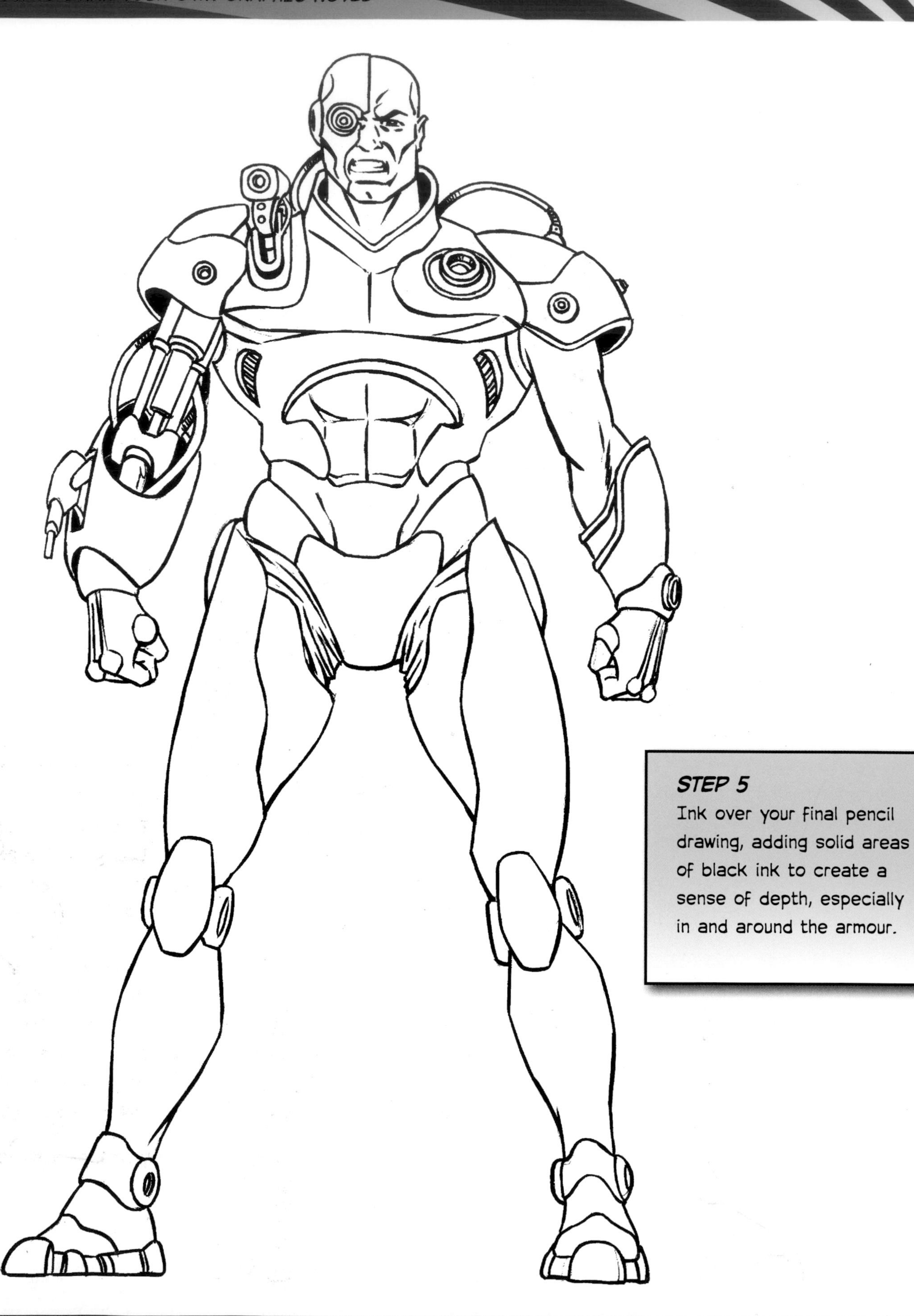

STEP 5

Ink over your final pencil drawing, adding solid areas of black ink to create a sense of depth, especially in and around the armour.

STEP 6

Finally, colour your character. The palette for this drawing uses contrasting tones to help distinguish between areas of flesh and those of metal. Warmer tones work for the skin, and cold, metallic blues and greys are best for the armour.

Animated Heroes

The Blue Comet

This character is drawn in a different art style. You may be familiar with this slick, stylized look from animated superhero programmes on TV.

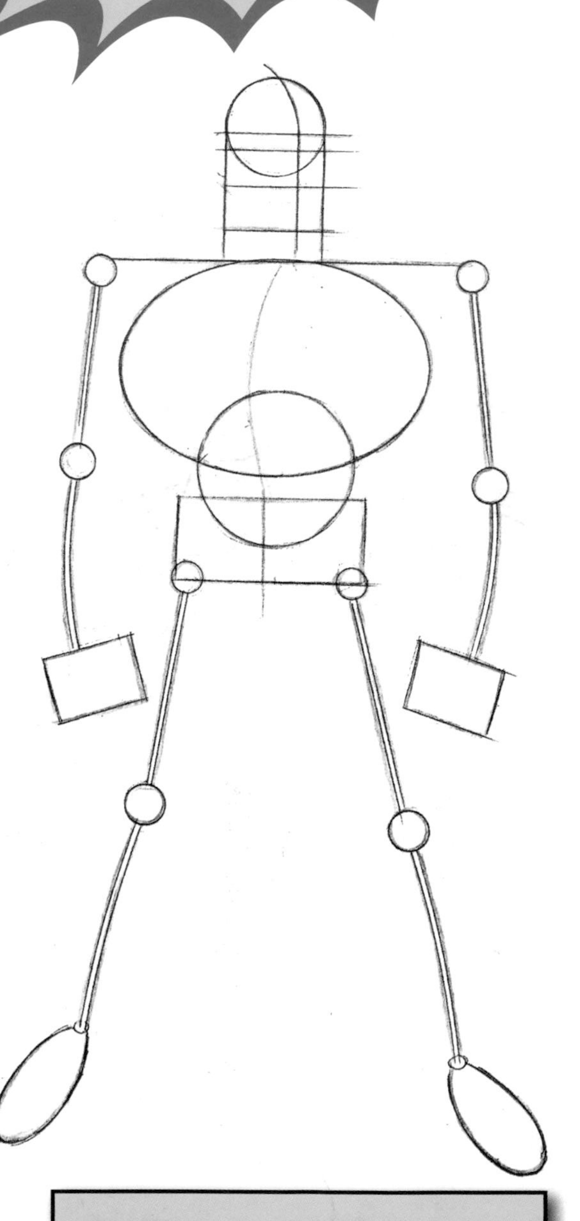

STEP 1

Start with some simple shapes fixed to a basic frame.

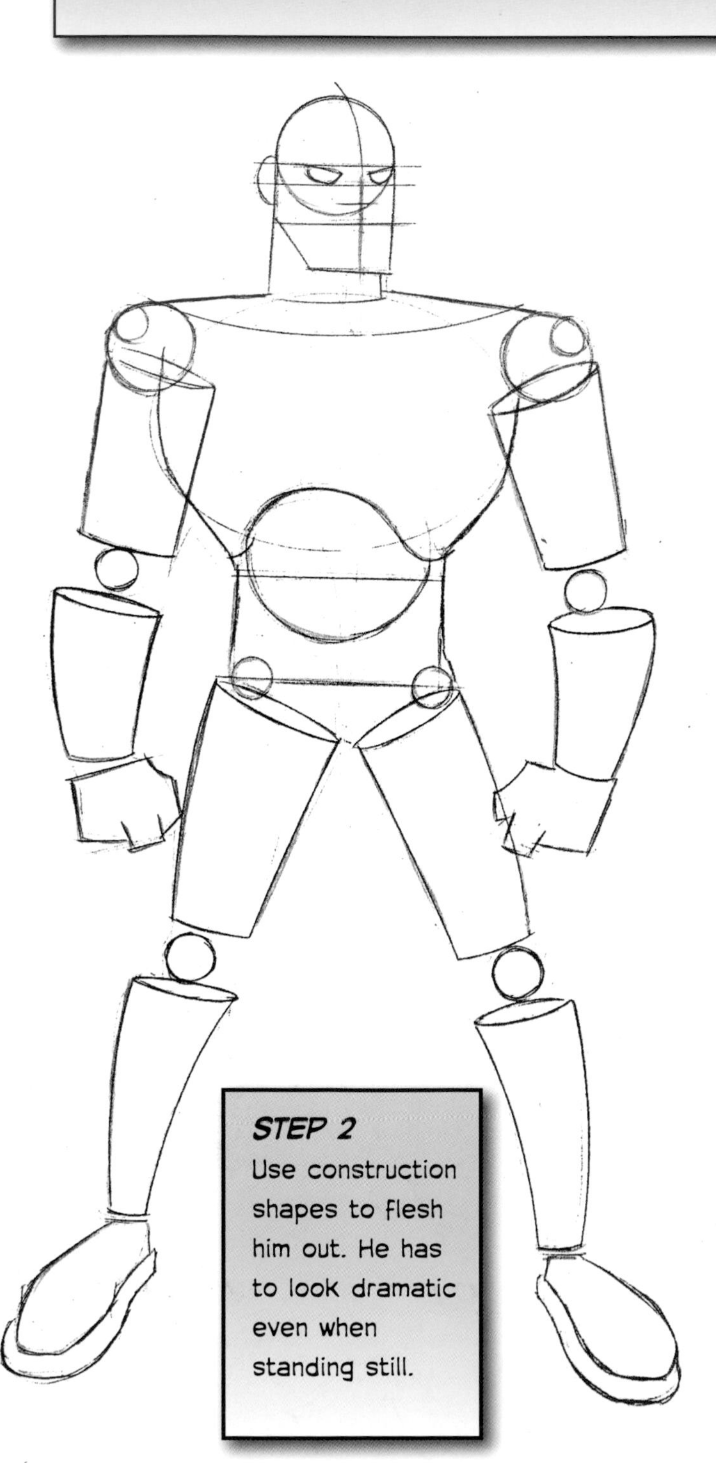

STEP 2

Use construction shapes to flesh him out. He has to look dramatic even when standing still.

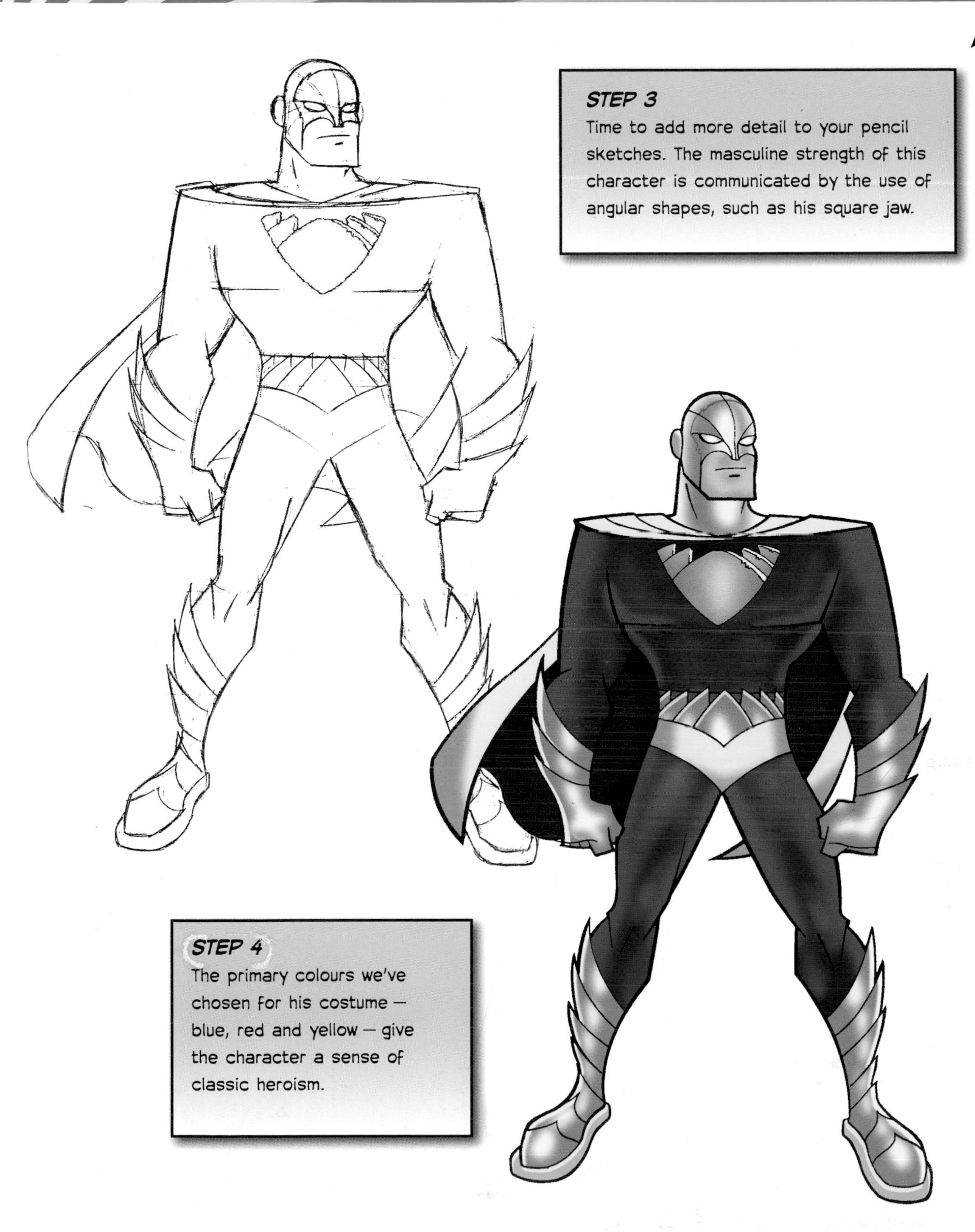

STEP 3

Time to add more detail to your pencil sketches. The masculine strength of this character is communicated by the use of angular shapes, such as his square jaw.

STEP 4

The primary colours we've chosen for his costume – blue, red and yellow – give the character a sense of classic heroism.

Rocket Girl

Don't be fooled into thinking that 'animated' style superhero art is super easy! You still need to think about how the shapes that make up the body fit together, and follow the same steps of pencilling, inking and colouring.

STEP 1

Build up this character from a series of circles and oval shapes.

STEP 2

To create dynamic action poses such as this one, you could try posing in front of the mirror.

STEP 3
Use thin lines for detail and a thicker line of ink around the outside of the figure. This will make her 'pop out' of the page.

STEP 4
The colours you choose will put across the character's personality. Colours like purple and green suggest that a hero is an unpredictable wild card.

Supporting Characters

Ordinary Joe

Will your hero have a partner? Comic-book sidekicks often have different skills or knowledge from the main heroes and act as their support. They might have to act as the voice of reason if the heroes go too far.

Loose Cannon

This swashbuckling character is the opposite of the voice of reason. He can spice up the dynamic of a story.

Supporting Heroine

Why not choose a strong female to be your supporting heroine? You wouldn't want to mess with this tough secret agent!

Warrior Sidekick

A sidekick like this could help out your hero when the going gets tough.

GLOSSARY

construction shapes Shapes, such as blocks and balls, that are drawn over a stick figure to make it more three-dimensional.

crime comics A type of graphic novel in which realistic criminals are hunted down (and often caught) by a hero or heroine. Often the hero is a private detective or police officer.

fantasy art Graphic novel illustrations that focus on imaginary magical or supernatural themes.

ink wash Ink (often watered down) that is used to colour an area of a figure or background.

layouts Sketches that show where items, such as figures and words, will be positioned on each page.

mystical arts Areas of magical knowledge.

primary colours The colours red, yellow and blue. These colours can be mixed together to make a range of other colours.

realism An art style that shows real life rather than an imaginary or fantastical world.

science fiction (sci-fi) Stories set in a future world, often involving time travel or travelling through space.

stick figure A simple drawing of a person using sticks and circles.

FURTHER READING

Bryan Hitch's Ultimate Comics Studio by Bryan Hitch (Impact, 2010)

The DC Comics Guide to Digitally Drawing Comics by Freddie E Wiliams II (Watson-Guptill, 2009)

Fantastic Four Visionaries, Volume 1 by John Byrne (Marvel Comics, 2001)

How to Draw Comic Book Heroes and Villains by Christopher Hart (Watson-Guptill, 2001)

How to Draw Johto Heroes by Ron Zalme (Scholastic, 2010)

WEBSITES

Drawing Comics and Anime
www.drawcomics.net

Drawing Comics: Video Tutorials
http://www.ehow.com/video_4754254_draw-comics.html

Drawing Manga: Video Tutorials
http://www.youtube.com/user/markcrilley

INDEX

animated heroes 24, 26
armour 21, 22, 23

barbarian warrior 6
brushwork 5

caped superhero 7
characters 6, 8, 9, 10, 11, 12, 16, 18, 20, 23, 24, 25, 26, 28
circle template 4
classic heroism 25
clothing 13, 17
colour 5, 15, 19, 23, 25, 26, 27
comic books 7
commando 7
computers 5
construction shapes 12, 20, 24
cops 11
crime comics 11
cyborg 6, 20

details 13, 17, 21, 25, 27
digital illustration 5
drawing 5, 13, 14, 21, 22, 23

face 12, 16, 20
fighting techniques 9
figure 12, 16, 20, 27
frame 12, 24
French curves 4

genre 6, 8, 11

hair 17
hands 16, 17
heroes 6, 7, 9, 10, 11, 12, 16, 19, 20, 24, 27, 28, 29
heroines 6, 10, 29

ink 5, 14, 22, 27

linework 5

martial-arts theme 9
muscles 12, 21
mystical arts 8

outline 12, 13, 16

paper 4–5
pencil drawing 13, 14, 21, 22
pencils 5
pens 5
pose 12, 20, 26

realism 11

science fiction (sci-fi) 7
secret agent 29
sidekicks 28, 29
sorceress 8, 16
stick figure 12, 16, 20
superhero 7, 8, 10, 24
superheroine 16
supporting characters 28

teenager 10
tools 4–5

warlock 8
warrior 6, 8, 12
weaponry 21
werewolf 10
Wild West 11
wizard 6, 8